Try Not To Laugh™ Challenge

Sassy Lassy

EDITION

Copyright© 2018 by Try Not to Laugh Challenge Joke Group

ALL RIGHTS RESERVED. By purchase of this book, you have been licensed one copy for personal use only. No part of this work may be reproduced, redistributed, or used in any form or by any means without prior written permission of the publisher and copyright owner.

PRIZES!

$50 GIFT CARD

Think YOU can win our JOKE CONTEST?!?!

Try Not to Laugh Challenge is having a CONTEST to see who is the MOST HILARIOUS boy or girl in the USA.

Please have your parents email us your best **original** joke and you could win a $50 gift card to Amazon.

Here are the rules:

1. It must be funny. Please do not give us jokes that aren't funny. We get enough of those from our joke writers

2. It must be original. We have computers and we know how to use them.

3. No help from the parents. Plus, they aren't even that funny anyway!!

Email your best joke to:

tntlpublishing@gmail.com

Winners will be announced via email.

Try Not to Laugh Challenge Group

The Try Not To Laugh™ Challenge Instructions:

- Face your opponent.

- Take turns reading jokes out loud to each other. HINT: Funny faces & noises are fair game!

- When someone laughs the other person gains a point.

- Person to get to 3 points is named The Try Not to Laugh CHAMPION!

Sassy Lassy Jokes

What's a firefly's favorite dance?

The glitterbug.

Why did the boy in love have skinned knees?

He fell hard for a girl.

What does one flirtatious hat say to another?

I fedorya.

Why did Peter Pan fly to his island and leave without landing?

Someone had put up a sign: "Never Land."

Why did the carpenter go to the beauty salon?

He needed his nails done.

Why are eyeshadow, lipstick, and mascara never mad at each other?

Because they always make-up.

Why did Tinkerbelle haggle for her new dress?

She wanted a fairy low price.

Where do roses sleep at night?

In their flowerbed!

What flower is the best kisser?

Tulips

Why did the princess take a bath?

Because she wanted to be queen.

Why did the star want to
be an actress?

So it could shine.

Why was the shoe bad
at gymnastics?

She was a flip-flop.

What should you wear to a
tea party?

A t-shirt.

What's rain's favorite accessory?

A rainbow.

Where does a sink go to dance?

The Dish-co

Why do mermaids always
lose coin flips?

They always call tails.

How did the ballerina win the dance competition?

Her dancing was on pointe.

Why did the student kidnap the Queen?

Because she needed a ruler!

Why can't you drive a flower?

Because your legs are too short to reach the petals.

Why did Cinderella get the Prince?

She was a shoe-in!

How did the traveler describe
Repunzel's hair?

"It was a let down!"

What sport is a princess best at?

Playing ball!

Why was Mulan late for
her appointment?

Because Mushu kept dragon his feet!

What did the Beast say when he
was saved from his curse?

"Saved by the Belle!"

Why did Aladdin's magic flying carpet leave him?

Because it was tired of being treated like a doormat!

Why doesn't Sebastian the crab share his stuff with Ariel?

Because he's shellfish!

What was Ariel's job title when she began cleaning the coral reefs?

Mermaid!

Why is everything so dirty in Neverland?

Because it's covered in pixie dust!

Why was the princess in the emergency room?

Because she broke her crown!

What did the boy say when he tripped in front of his crush?

"I think I've fallen for you!"

Why did Mulan think her mirror was broken?

Because her reflection didn't show who she was inside!

What did Elsa say when Anna wouldn't stop complaining about her boyfriend?

"Let it go!"

What happened when the captain of a ship in Neverland started watching shows online?

He got hooked!

What did Aladdin say when the flying carpet flew too high?

"A whole new world!"

What's Sleeping Beauty's favorite thing to wear?

Pajamas!

How did Ariel describe her date with Prince Eric in the canoe?

"Boat loads of fun!"

What's a princess's favorite time?

Knight time!

How did Ariel feel when she left the ocean to walk on land?

Like a fish out of water!

What did one diamond necklace say to the other?

"You're a gem!"

Why did Genie get mad?

Because he was rubbed the wrong way!

Why doesn't Elsa care when she gets a brain freeze?

Because the cold never bothered her anyway!

Why didn't Tiana show up for work?

Because she had a frog in her throat!

How did the princess feel when she was swept off of her feet?

It was an uplifting experience!

What comment did Tinker Bell get on her magic test?

Fairy good job!

Why didn't Merida make it into the archery club?

She lost her shot!

Where is Sleeping Beauty's favorite place to be?

In bed!

Why did Cinderella look so good for the Prince's ball?

Because she knew how to clean up!

What kind of castle does the princess of the desert live in?

A sand castle!

What party game is Snow White best at?

Bobbing for apples!

What kind of toilet does a royal cat use?

A glitter box!

Why is Belle always expressing her love for reading?

Because she's an open book!

How did the Prince feel when he dropped Cinderella's glass slipper?

Shattered!

What is a cow's favorite Disney princess?

MOOlan

What is Elsa and Anna's favorite dessert?

Frozen yogurt.

What is a lion's favorite Disney princess?

A-ROAR-A (Aurora)

Why does everyone like playing games with Snow White?

Because she's the fairest one of all.

Which band never turns left or right?

One Direction

What did the fig tree buy for
its antsy kid?

A FIGet spinner.

What do you call an insect
with rhythm?

A beat bug.

What did the sparkles say to
the pixie dust?

Don't glitter, it's bad for the environment.

How does one ballerina
compliment another?

You're on pointe!

What's a ballerina's favorite
type of bread?

A bun.

Which flowers have mouths?

Two lips. (Tulips)

What is the Little Mermaid's
favorite letter?

D, because it's "Under the 'C'."

Which Disney princess do you get when you ask for more Anna?

Mo' Ana (Moana)

What happens when Jafar gets too close?

He becomes JaNEAR.

How did the pony know she was late getting home?

It was pasture bedtime.

What do ponies do when they fall in love?

They get mare-eed.

What is a pony's favorite cartoon?

Whinny-the-Pooh.

What does Cinderella wear when
she mows the lawn?

A grass slipper

What kind of computer is Snow White
afraid to use?

An Apple.

Why did the dancer lose the
dance competition?

Because she tapped out!

What did the sneaker say
to the stiletto heel?

"How's the weather up there?!"

Why couldn't Tiana marry the
frog prince?

Because he croaked!

What happened when Aladdin and
Jasmine went on magic carpet rides?

Their love soared to new heights!

What do you call a date
with Snow White?

A Snow day!

How did Tinker Bell feel when she got her wings polished?

Pretty fly!

What kind of dance was the frog prince best at?

Hip hop!

What happened to the princess' royal chair?

It got throne away!

What is Ariel's favorite kind of story?

She prefers a good fish-out-of-water tale!

Why is Princess Aurora always late for class?

Because she's trying to catch up on her beauty sleep.

What is Rapunzel's favorite piece of advice?

"Let your hair down."

What happened to the baseball glove that accidentally went through the spin cycle?

He was all washed up!

Why should you bring Merida to a scary movie?

Because she's brave.

How do unicorns warn each other about rough housing?

"It's all fun and games until someone loses an eye."

What did the astronomy teacher say to his students?

"Aim for the stars."

How do Pegasuses fly?

On a wing and a prayer.

What do bunnies like to do at the mall?

Shop 'til they hop!

Why didn't the little girl
like wearing diamonds?

She was too cool for jewels.

What is a fairy's favorite type
of haircut?

A pixie cut.

What should you do if you see
a pretty, fancy dress?

Don't cry over frilled silk.

Why did the ballerina get so much
praise after her recital?

Because her dancing was on pointe.

Which crayon is the funniest?

Tickle me pink

What did the ballerina's mom think of
her daughter's performance?

She was tutu delighted.

What's Elsa's favorite game?

Freeze tag.

What do you call the royal feline
owned by a princess?

An aristocat.

What do you call a flower that has learned to fly?

An upsy-daisy.

How did the surgeon win over the girl?

He touched her heart!

How did the beauty school student do on her manicure test?

She nailed it!

What did the girl say to the boy after stealing his lollipop?

"Sucker!"

Silly Jokes

Why did the Headless Horseman study so much?

He wanted to get a-head.

What is corn's favorite music?

Pop.

What is Anthony Davis' favorite type of festivity?

A block party.

Why do Legos figures never get married?

They're too easy to break apart.

Why did the knife smell bad?

It couldn't stop cutting the cheese.

What do electricians say when
they see a sunset?

Lights out.

What did the cowboy say
to the artist?

Draw.

If a king and a queen are a pair when
sitting on a throne, what are they
when sitting on a toilet?

A Royal Flush.

A student pilot was on her first training flight with her flight instructor. "How do you fly this thing?", She asked him. The instructor replied, "I just wing it."

Why can't Monday lift Saturday?

It's a weak day.

What did the string say to the scissors when they were sitting in traffic?

"Don't cut me off!"

Why was the politician out of breath?

He was running for office.

Why didn't the window have
anything to do?

His schedule was all clear.

Why did the army recruit not
understand his commander's
instructions?

He was being too general.

Why did the wife kick the fisherman
out of the house?

He was being crabby.

What did the happy proton say
to the sad electron?

"Just be positive!"

What do you call a
substitute musician?

Band-Aid.

Why did the opera singer's pants
fall down?

He was belting it out.

Why do park benches always yawn?

They're so board.

Why couldn't the arrow make
any friends?

It was alwas pointing at people.

Why did the maid plant trees
inside the house?

She was asked to spruce up.

How much does lightning weigh?

Not much. It's light.

What is a soccer player's favorite
chemical element?

Goooooooooooooold!

Why did the dog punch the
punching bag?

He was a boxer!

Why did the bear go to the riverbank?

Could you imagine what would happen if a bear used a bank in the middle of town?

Why do jewelers love to vacation on Saturn?

To see its rings.

Why did the fastest cat in class get kicked out of school?

He was a cheetah.

Which state has the greatest number of jokes?

Punnsylvania.

Name a bone that is found outside
the body of certain musicians?

Trombone.

Why did the train crack up pulling
into the station?

It was loco!

What did the geometry teacher drive
to school every day?

A boxcar.

What does a mule use to get
into the barn?

A donkey.

When Dave drove to work, it never cost him money. Why?

He used the freeway.

What can you say about Paul and Pat when they squeezed into the tiny spacecraft?

They were like two P's in a pod!

Where is the best place to sit when a submarine is diving?

Inside.

Why did the lawyer show up in court in his underwear?

He forgot his lawsuit!

What should you do if you bite off
more than you can chew?

Spit it out.

Why are geologists trying
to mine clouds?

Every cloud has a silver lining.

Why was Alexander Graham's
invention of the telephone
a waste of time?

He could have heard everything through the
grapevine!

Which is the happiest capital
in the U.S.?

Annapolis, the capital of MERRY-LAND!

Which U.S. state begins with
the letter Y?

Y-O-Ming.

Why was the teenager no longer
allowed online without a license?

He crashed the computer.

How did the mother plant know her
son would love gymnastics?

He was a tumbleweed!

What do you call it when somebody
stumbles and falls on a grassy area?

A field trip!

How do you know the teeth were excited when they got braces?

They were wired!

What type of musical group likes to wrap itself around its music?

A rubber band!

What's a ball that you don't throw, shoot, eat, spit, bounce, or catch?

Eyeball!

Why did the scissors kick the joke out of the book?

It didn't make the cut.

What do turtles, eggs, and beaches all have?

Shells.

What did the mom say when she found out her son had been shuffling his feet on the carpet and zapping everyone with a static electric charge?

"His behavior is shocking!"

The toilet paper was getting close to the end of its life. The nearby towel shouted, "Get out of there before it's all over for you!" What did the toilet paper reply?

"I can't quit yet. I'm on a roll!"

If amusement park candy had a choice, from what material would their wrappers be made?

Cotton, of course. Whoever heard of eating polyester candy?

Matt went over to Dee's house to watch an opera on TV. He asked her why she told him to bring soap. What did she reply?

"Because we're watching a Soap Opera!"

What did the bridge say to the ship as the engineer raised both sides?

"It's a draw!

A man was upset because his favorite shirt had a lot of wrinkles, and he needed it for work that day. He took the shirt to the dry cleaners. What did the woman who worked there say?

"Don't worry, we'll iron things out."

Why did the washing machine feel sore?

Because it had been running for over an hour!

Why was the remote controller so happy?

Because someone pushed "Play!"

What is the lightest type of coat
to wear?

A White One!

Why did the man drop his phone and
grab his chair with both hands?

Because the person on the phone said:
"Please hold."

What did the tent say when it
got arrested?

It said: "You set me up!"

What time of year do people get
injured the most?

In the fall.

Why did the quarterback take the hardest classes?

Because he knew he would pass.

What do you call a porcupine with no ears?

It doesn't matter what you call him: he won't hear you anyway.

Why didn't the shopkeeper follow when his customer went down the left aisle?

Because the customer is always right.

Why did the king tell his servants not to smudge his drawing?

Because he wanted to preserve his line.

Why are police officers such good dancers?

Because they are always on the beat.

What do golfers and truck drivers have in common?

They are both good at long drives.

When is it dangerous to go to the stock exchange?

When prices drop.

Where is the best place to be?

In first place!

Why did the criminal bring a maid to the music store?

Because he wanted a clean record.

Why did the marathoners abduct the movie star?

Because they wanted to take the lead.

Why did the manager put bricks under his staff's chair legs?

Because they asked for a raise.

Did you hear about the guy who was attacked by a sandblaster?

It was a heavy blow.

Why did the father drop his son's stereo?

Because the music was too heavy.

Did you hear about the illustrator who ran for President?

He really wanted to make his mark.

Why didn't the scientist's theory about light make sense?

Because it wasn't sound.

Why did the musician throw away her table?

Because it was flat.

What did the train engine say when the caboose said something confusing?

"I don't follow."

Why wouldn't the hermit crab give the mollusk a ride on his shell?

Because he didn't want to pull a mussel.

Why did the construction worker take a pen to work?

He had to fill in the concrete forms.

Did you hear what happened to the guy who always looked behind him because was afraid of mailmen?

One day, he accidentally ran into the post.

Why wouldn't the limousine talk
to the coupe?

She wouldn't date anyone so short.

Why is it a bad idea to argue with
a pair of pliers?

Because they always try to twist everything.

Why didn't the cube admit that it
should become a pyramid?

Because it didn't want to lose face.

Why did the American hit the British
shopkeeper?

Because the shopkeeper said:
"That will be one pound."

Why did the news channel keep showing videos of a large spinning object?

Because that was their top story.

Why didn't the girl respond when she heard a magical voice coming from the water where she threw her coin?

Because she doesn't speak well.

What did the zombie dad say when his zombie son told him he didn't want to be a zombie anymore?

He said: "You're dead to me," and he gave him a hug.

What did the lake say to the ocean when they were talking philosophy?

It said: "Wow, that's deep."

Why didn't the farmer's son study medicine?

Because he wanted to go into a different field.

Why was the smelter worker careful to follow all of the safety procedures?

Because he didn't want to get fired.

Why did the miner get chosen first by the team captain?

Because the captain wanted the best pick.

Why didn't the man follow the directions to assemble the stairs?

Because he couldn't get past the first step.

Why didn't the investor keep putting money into his laundry business?

Because the whole thing was a wash.

What is the math teacher's favorite dessert?

Pi

Made in the USA
San Bernardino, CA
19 November 2019

60145838R00039